Relax Kids:
Be Brilliant

52 Positive Activities for Kids

Relax Kids:
Be Brilliant

52 Positive Activities for Kids

Marneta Viegas

OUR STREET
BOOKS

Winchester, UK
Washington, USA

First published by Our Street Books, 2014
Our Street Books is an imprint of John Hunt Publishing Ltd., Laurel House, Station Approach,
Alresford, Hants, SO24 9JH, UK
office1@jhpbooks.net
www.johnhuntpublishing.com
www.ourstreet-books.com

For distributor details and how to order please visit the 'Ordering' section on our website.

Text copyright: Marneta Viegas 2014

ISBN: 978 1 78279 237 6

A CIP catalogue record for this book is available from the British Library.

Printed and bound by CPI Group (UK) Ltd, Croydon, CR0 4YY

We operate a distinctive and ethical publishing philosophy in all areas of our business, from our global network of
authors to production and worldwide distribution.

Your smile is a radiance that brightens the world!

relax Kids
www.relaxkids.com

When you grin, you create a beam that brings joy and light to others.

relax Kids
www.relaxkids.com

If you believe, you can achieve.

relax Kids
www.relaxkids.com

You are Awesome!

relax Kids
www.relaxkids.com

Be kind to yourself and remember everyday that you are amazing!

relax Kids
www.relaxkids.com

You have so many gifts and talents.

relax Kids
www.relaxkids.com

You are amazing!

relax Kids
www.relaxkids.com

I can see you are a fast learner.

relax Kids
www.relaxkids.com

You are very intelligent and can do whatever you focus your mind on.

relax Kids
www.relaxkids.com

WELL DONE! Keep it up!

relax Kids
www.relaxkids.com

You are superb.

relax Kids
www.relaxkids.com

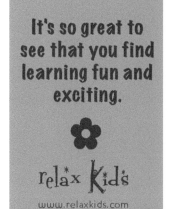

It's so great to see that you find learning fun and exciting.

relax Kids
www.relaxkids.com

Believe in yourself and your abilities.

relax Kids
www.relaxkids.com

You are remarkable.

relax Kids
www.relaxkids.com

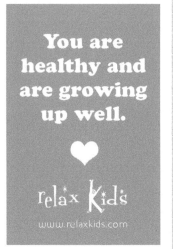

You are healthy and are growing up well.

relax Kids
www.relaxkids.com

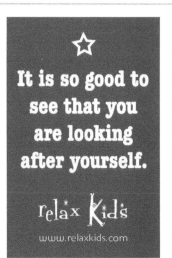

It is so good to see that you are looking after yourself.

relax Kids
www.relaxkids.com

You are
Extraordinary!

relax Kids
www.relaxkids.com

You are so
unique and so
special and
loved by
everyone

relax Kids
www.relaxkids.com

Everyone
loves you for
who you are

relax Kids
www.relaxkids.com

You are
Incredible

relax Kids
www.relaxkids.com

It is so great
to see that
you enjoy
being, feeling
and thinking
positive

relax Kids
www.relaxkids.com

You are so
determined
and
dedicated.

relax Kids
www.relaxkids.com

You are
getting more
and more
confident
every day.

relax Kids
www.relaxkids.com

It is fantastic to
watch how
brilliant you are.

relax Kids
www.relaxkids.com

Every day gets
better and
better for you.

relax Kids
www.relaxkids.com

You are
Triumphant.

relax Kids
www.relaxkids.com

You are full
of love and
everyone
loves you.

relax Kids
www.relaxkids.com

You will always
have lots of
friends because
you are kind
and friendly

relax Kids
www.relaxkids.com

You are
Wonderful.

relax Kids
www.relaxkids.com

Every day in every
way you are getting
better and better

relax Kids
www.relaxkids.com

Never give up,
you can do
whatever you
want to do.

relax Kids
www.relaxkids.com

**You are
Terrific.**

relax Kids
www.relaxkids.com

Relax Kids Positivity Bank

Print out and cut up our Relax Kids bank notes for kindness, sharing and good behaviour. Make a Positivity Bank and be rewarded with the bank notes when you do something good. At the end of the month, open your Positivity Bank and count up the notes you have collected. Jot them down on your Positivity table and see if you can beat your amount next time!

How to make your Bank

Don't forget to print out your Relax Kids bank notes of positivity!

You will need:
Shoe box with lid
Paint, pens etc.
Sheet of acetate or similar plastic
Sticky tape

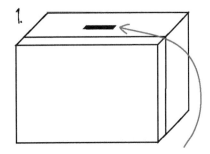

1.

You will need to start by carefully cutting a thin rectangle (big enough to post your bank notes into) in the middle of the long side of the box

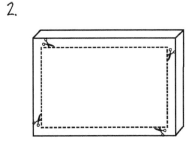

2.

Next you will need to cut a rectangle out of the lid – leave about 3cm around the edge. Paint and decorate your box inside and out

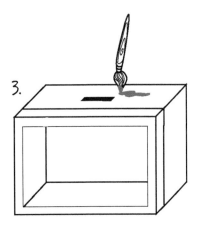

3.

Then decorate and paint the box inside and out. When it is fully dry, you will need to tape the sheet of acetate to the inside of the lid, filling the reactangle you've cut out.

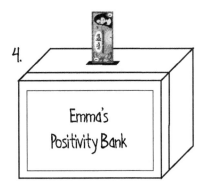

4.

Emma's
Positivity Bank

Write your name and Positivity Bank' on the acetate with a pen or cut out the letters in coloured paper and stick on.

relax Kids

you are a
shining star
who spreads
rays of
happiness

relax kids
www.relaxkids.com

you are a
special star
who sparkles
with joy

relax kids
www.relaxkids.com

you are a
lucky & lovely
star who will
always be ok

relax kids
www.relaxkids.com

you are a
helpful star who
always
always
supports others

relax kids
www.relaxkids.com

you are an
amazing star
who shines
with so many
talents

relax kids
www.relaxkids.com

you   are
a loving star
with a huge
heart

relax kids
www.relaxkids.com

you are a
brilliant star
who always
does their
best

relax kids
www.relaxkids.com

you are a
kind star
who always
lends a hand

relax kids
www.relaxkids.com

you are a
friendly star
who can get on
with everyone

relax kids
www.relaxkids.com

you are a happy
star who makes
everyone smile

relax kids
www.relaxkids.com

you are a
beautiful star
who radiates
with love and
happiness

relax kids
www.relaxkids.com

you are a gentle
star who thinks
of others first

relax kids
www.relaxkids.com

Aware-Ness

Calm-Ness

Cheery-Ness

Brave-Ness

Cool-Ness

Forgive-Ness

Friendly-Ness

Happy-Ness

Animal Eggs

You will need:
Eggs
Large needle
Paint/felt tip pens
Coloured paper/card
Craft Glue
Pipe cleaners/small pom balls etc.

1 First, you will need to blow out your eggs. Over a bowl, carefully puncture the egg shell with the needle and gently make the hole slightly bigger than the width of the needle. Push the needle all the way into the egg so that it breaks the yolk inside. Make a small hole at the opposite end and you'll need to blow through this hole so that it blows out the egg out of the slightly larger hole at the other end into the bowl. Carefully wash the egg with cold water and dry.

2 Think about what animal you would like to make and then paint your egg or colour it with felt tip pens - is your animal one solid colour or does it have a pattern?

3 Once dry, you'll need to add your animal's feet/nose/wings/tail/ears etc. Glue on the poms for the feet (or you could even cut out feet from thick card) and glue onto the bottom. Glue on wings, ears etc. out of coloured card. You could use pie cleaners for tails which you can poke into the hole in the egg. Use black felt tip to draw on whiskers, eyes or any other details.

Here are some animal egg ideas -

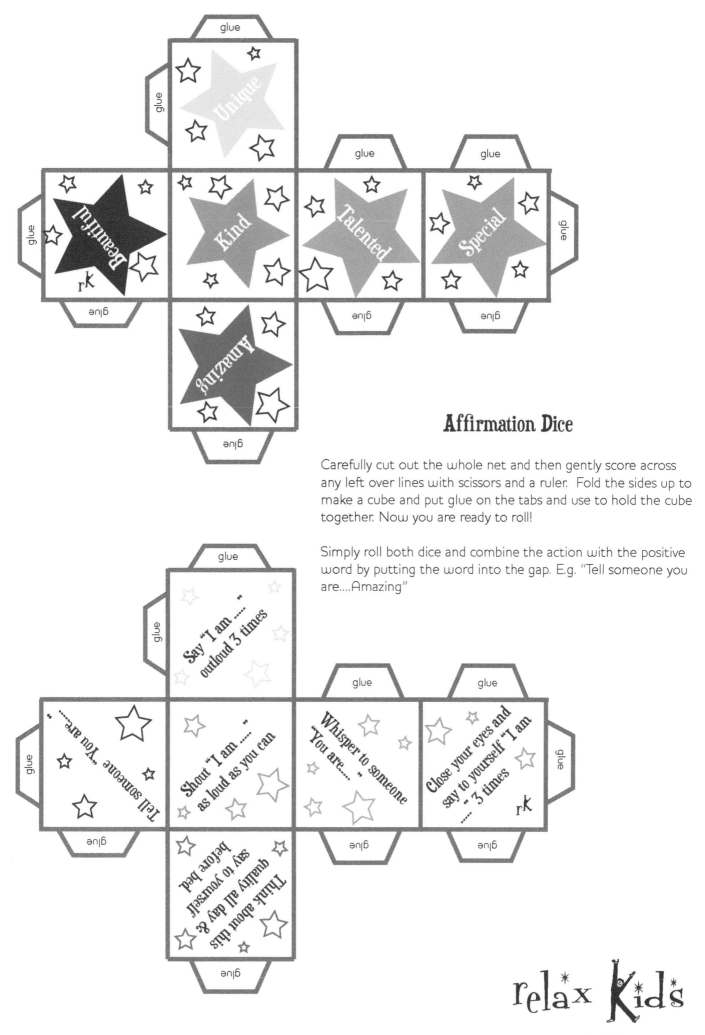

Affirmation Dice

Carefully cut out the whole net and then gently score across any left over lines with scissors and a ruler. Fold the sides up to make a cube and put glue on the tabs and use to hold the cube together. Now you are ready to roll!

Simply roll both dice and combine the action with the positive word by putting the word into the gap. E.g. "Tell someone you are....Amazing"

Dice 1 (words)

- Unique
- Beautiful
- Kind
- Talented
- Special
- Amazing

Dice 2 (actions)

- Say "I am ......" outloud 3 times
- Tell someone "You are....."
- Shout "I am ....." as loud as you can
- Whisper to someone "You are....."
- Close your eyes and say to yourself "I am ....." 3 times
- Think about this quality all day & say to yourself before bed

relax Kids

www.relaxkids.com

CIRQUE DE CROSSWORD

DOWN
1. An animal which you can ride (5)
2. Work together as a .... (4)
3. A person who works in a circus may be called a performer or an .... (11)
4. You may describe an acrobat as this ....(7)
5. Fabric shelter (4)
6. All the circus performers walk around the arena together in a .... (6)
7. Acrobats are very .... (8)
8. Throwing and catching, you are a .... (7)
9. You are clumsy which makes people laugh .... (5)

ACROSS
11. This walker balances on a .... (9)
4. Flexible, amazing and very talented .... (7)
12. A very large animal with a long trunk (8)
13. Ready to catch them in they fall, a safety .... (3)
14. A swing very high up (7)
9. What this crossword is about (6)
15. Another place where you might find 12. across (3)
16. The main circus tent is called a .... (6)
17. Clowns are .... (5)
18. Team leader of the entire circus (10)

www.relaxkids.com

Coupons to give Mum & Dad

relax Kids www.relaxkids.com

This coupon entitles you to one

1 hour of peace & quiet

Expiry:............................
Signed:............................

relax Kids

This coupon entitles you to one

Breakfast in bed

Expiry:............................
Signed:............................

relax Kids

This coupon entitles you to one

Bedroom tidy

Expiry:............................
Signed:............................

relax Kids

This coupon entitles you to one

Washing up duty

Expiry:............................
Signed:............................

relax Kids

This coupon entitles you to one

Big hug

Expiry:............................
Signed:............................

relax Kids

This coupon entitles you to one

List of things that make you wonderful!

Expiry:............................
Signed:............................

relax Kids

This coupon entitles you to one

Day of making mum feel speical

Expiry:............................
Signed:............................

relax Kids

This coupon entitles you to one

Day of making dad feel speical

Expiry:............................
Signed:............................

relax Kids

This coupon entitles you to one

Helping make dinner

Expiry:............................
Signed:............................

relax Kids

Jellyfish Craft

You will need: Paper plates/bowls/cups
Paint
Ribbons, strips of fabric, wool etc.
Glue - such as PVA
Needle & Thread

 Paint the outside of you paper bowl or plate and the inside of another.

 When the paint is dry, coat the inside of the bowl/plate which has been painted on the outside with glue. Stick some ribbons around the edges on the bowl or plate before sticking down the other bowl or plate (painted inside) into the other,

 Gather together varying lengths of ribbon/wool/fabric/paper. You may need an adult for this next step - poke a hole through the top on the bowl/plate with the needle. Hold in place the middle of the strips of ribbon etc that you've gathered. Loop through strong thread or fishing line over the strips and back up through the hole to the top (you may wish to loop round afew times to make sure it's secure).

 Leave an amount of thread/fishing line you require out of the the top so that you have enough to hang from the ceiling. The last little job is to add some fun, googly eyes which you can make and stick of with paper.

www.relaxkids.com

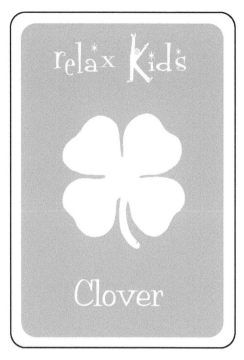

Clover

Black Cat

Star

Coin

Horse Shoe

Heather

Seven

Crystal Ball

relax Kids

www.relaxkids.com

Snap - Lay out all the cards face down in front of all the players. Take it in turns to flip over two cards at a time. If the two cards are the same, the player keeps that pair. If the two cards do not match, they are turned face down again and it's the next player's turn. The player with the most pairs at the end is the winner.

Memory - Lay all the cards on the table. On each turn, the player will first turn one card over, then a second. If the two cards match, the player scores one point, the two cards are removed from the game, and the player gets another turn. If they do not match, the cards are turned back over. The winner is the one with the most pairs.

Design you own crest

How to design your own crest:
Write down your values, draw symbols and add a motto that represents you and your life.

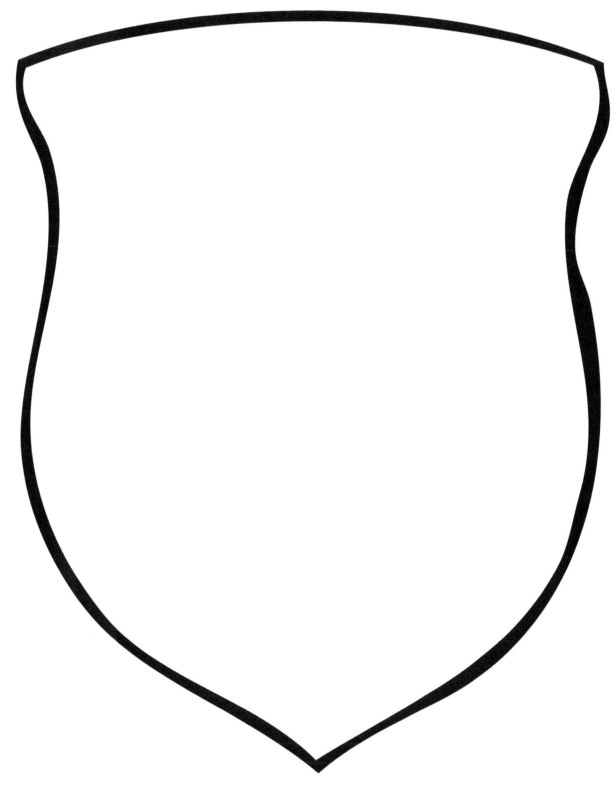

WORRY WALL

WRITE ALL YOUR WORRIES ON THE WORRY WALL

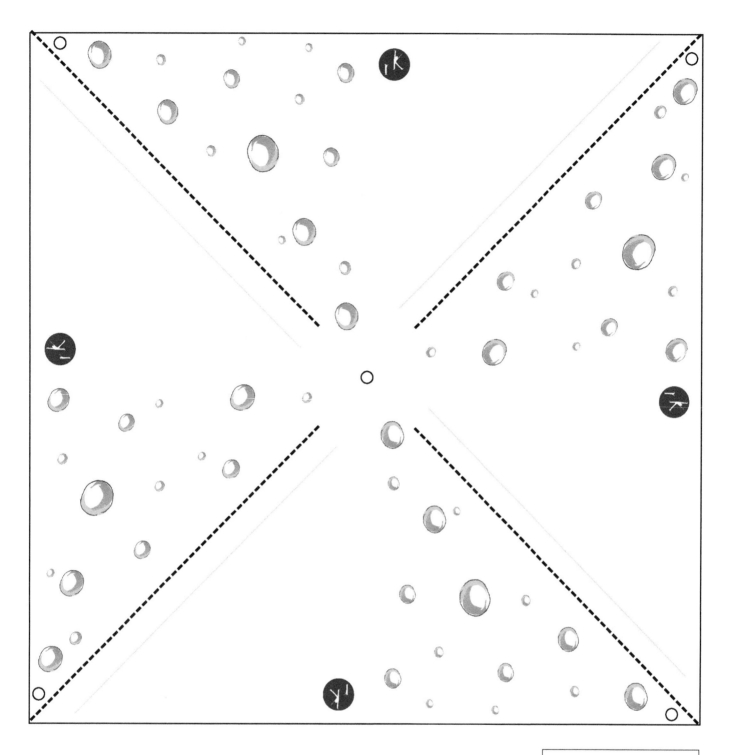

Affirmation Windmill

Before making the windmilll, first write a postive affirmation on each section on the grey line. You can colour these in if you wish and make them look beautiful!

Now you are ready to make your windmill. Cut around square and along the dashed lines. Make holes where the black circles are in the corners and centre - to do this, carefully push through a split pin with s lump of plasticine the other side. Fold in the corners with the holes to the centre and then carefully join all the corners together with the split-pin. Add a straw or stick to the back either with a lump of plasticne or using the split-pin to wrap around it.

Now your Affirmation Windmill is ready! Gently blow your positive thoughts and affirmations around the windmill.

fortune cookies

Ingredients:

2 large egg whites
1 teaspoon vanilla essence
3 tablespoons vegetable or olive oil
8 tablespoons plain flour
8 tablespoons granulated sugar

1½ teaspoons cornstarch
(custard powder works great too!)
¼ teaspoon salt
2 teaspoons water

Preheat oven to 150°

Method:

1. Grease 2 large baking trays and line with greaseproof paper. (reusable baking paper is best as it makes it the cookies very easy to lift off the baking sheet).

2. Beat the egg whites, vanilla and oil until frothy but not stiff.

3. Sift the flour, salt, sugar and cornstarch into a seperate bowl. Stir the water into the flour mixture.

4. Add the flour mixture to the eggs and stir until you have a smooth batter.

5. Place level tablespoons of the batter onto your baking sheets, spacing them at least 10cm apart. Gently tilt the baking sheet until the batter spreads to form circles about 8cm in diameter.

6. Bake for 12-14 minutes or until the outer rims of the cookies are golden brown.

7. Working quickly, remove from the oven and lift using a spatula or palette knife. Flip the cookie over and place a folded fortune in the centre. Fold the cookie in half and using the glass bend the cookie downwards either side of the rim the glass. They won't take long to set into shape.

Cut out these fortunes to place inside your fortune cookies.

I see a heart on your horizon - you will always be loved	I see a flower on your horizon - you will always be beautiful
I see a star on your horizon - you will always use your talents	I see a mountain on your horizon - you will always be strong
I see a four leaf clover on your horizon - you will always be lucky	I see a cloud on your horizon - you will always have peace
I see a sun on your horizon - you will always be happy	I see a moon on your horizon - you will always stay cool
I see a purse on your horizon - you will be rich	I see a book on your horizon - you will always be wise
I see a bird on your horizon - you will always be free	I see two hands on your horizon - you will always have friends

Make Your Own Relax Kids Mr (or Mrs!) Grass Head

You will need: Pair of old tights/stockings
Grass seeds
Potting soil
Empty yoghurt pot
Elastic band
Glue
Scissors
Googlie eyes/decorating materials

1. Cut about 20cm off the end of your stocking (with the toe bit) so it should look like a sock.

2. Stretch the stocking over a mug or something similar. Put it about 2 teaspoons of grass seeds and then fill the rest with soil so that it is a neat ball.

3. Tie a knot in the end of the stocking - keep any excess at the end.

4. To make a nose, pinch a large part of soil and stocking in the middle and wrap the elastic band around tightly.

5. Glue on googlie eyes. Draw or stick on lips, eyebrows, glasses or whatever else you would like for your Mr/Mrs Grass head.

6. Your Grass Head is going to sit in the empty yoghurt pot. It's going to help keep it watered, stop it from rolling around but you can also decorate like it's the body of your Grass head. You can 'dress' it any way you like or you can cut out and stick on the Relax Kids t-shirt.

7. When you are ready, fill the yoghurt pot half full with water. Place your Mr/Mrs Grass head on top (the excess stocking should soak up the water up the head) and give it a little water on top of his/her head.

Place in a well lit area like a sunny windowsill and water regularly. Watch his/her hair grow and give hair cuts when needed!

relax Kids

www.relaxkids.com

Serene Swan

Tolerent Tree

Radiant Rose

Super Star

Optimistic Owl

Floating Feather

Tremendous Tresure

Spectacular Sun

Reliable Rainbow

Truthful Tortoise

Charming Cake

Wonderful Wizard

Magical Garden Wordsearch

```
R  H  X  D  E  K  B  E  N  M  Y  H  D  G  I  V
W  T  O  A  D  S  T  O  O  L  K  M  W  J  H  P
F  U  F  I  G  Q  I  I  H  K  A  E  V  S  C  D
P  S  H  S  G  T  X  D  N  G  V  C  T  N  R  A
R  V  W  Y  A  N  E  K  K  R  G  O  N  O  O  F
O  D  M  N  H  R  F  Q  V  C  N  U  E  W  H  F
S  U  R  A  L  L  I  P  R  E  T  A  C  D  T  O
E  A  Q  R  B  Z  O  M  M  P  V  U  P  R  U  D
C  L  T  O  T  L  V  T  O  M  C  N  R  O  L  I
Y  M  X  R  V  D  E  N  F  U  Q  P  S  P  I  L
M  O  K  C  P  G  D  R  I  B  Y  D  A  L  P  R
P  S  R  J  R  P  W  S  U  Y  R  I  A  F  O  C
L  U  C  O  O  G  B  L  U  E  B  E  L  L  E  S
T  T  F  M  B  U  M  B  L  E  B  E  E  H  J  N
T  C  B  L  Q  C  S  T  L  D  Y  B  J  J  G  Y
```

bluebell	daffodil
ladybird	snowdrop
bumblebee	daisy
orchid	toadstool
carnation	fairy
pond	tulip
caterpillar	forget me not
rose	waterlily

www.relaxkids.com

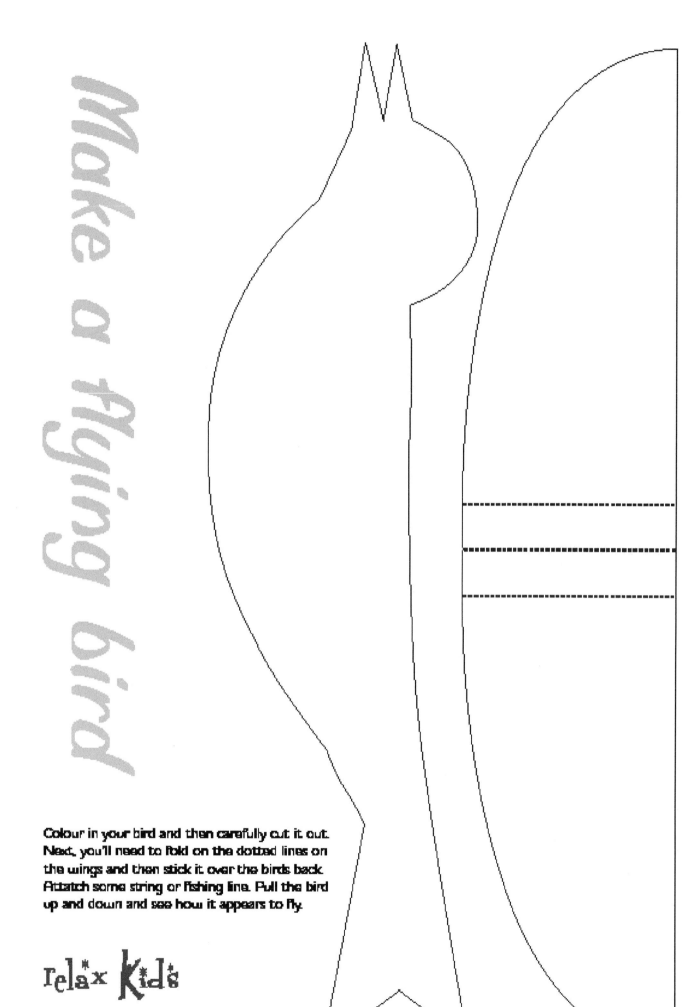

Make a flying bird

Colour in your bird and then carefully cut it out.
Next, you'll need to fold on the dotted lines on
the wings and then stick it over the birds back.
Attatch some string or fishing line. Pull the bird
up and down and see how it appears to fly.

relax Kids

www.relaxkids.com

relax kids

www.relaxkids.com

First, colour in your mask. Draw two circles where you eyes will be and carefully cut them out. Cut out the mask. You're mask is nearly ready - either tape a straw at the back or carefully make two holes either side and tie on some elastic.

Origami

Origami is the Japanese art of paperfolding. "Ori" is the Japanese word for folding and "kami" is the Japanese word for paper. It was originally invented in China which later came over to Japan. Years ago paper was very expensive so was something really only for the rich, however as the years went on and paper got cheaper, more and more people, rich and poor, were able to enjoy the art of paperfolding.

For these origami folds, you will need squared, coloured or patterened paper. Origami paper is best (coloured one side, blank the other)

Fan

Fold up the bottom of the paper about 1.5cm then turn the paper over and do the same. Cotinue these steps until you have run out of paper to fold. Once you have reached the end, pull open slightly and the pinch the end about 5cm from the bottom. Spread out the top further to reveal your beautiful fan

Cup

These cups are very practical. Can be used to hold pens, sweets, flowers and anything else you can think of!

1. Start with a square piece of paper of any size (however big or small you want your cup). Fold in half and join the corners together to make a triangle.

2. Pull the right corner across to the opposite side but keeping the top of the new fold straight and horizontal.

3. Repeat with the left side so that it goes over on top of your previous fold.

4. You should be left with a triangle on top. Split this and fold the front one forward and the one behind back.

5. Now, stick your finger in the middle and gently squeeze the outside edges to pop it in shape of a cup.

Sampan or Boat

1. Start with your square paper (colour side down if it is like origami paper) and you will need to fold it corner to corner diagonally aswell as folding it in half vertically and horizontally.

2. Fold up the top and bottom sides to meet the crease in the middle.

3. Fold in the four corners, again to meet the crease in the centre. They should look like little triangles.

4. Take the bottom left corner and fold it up the the centre crease again however this triangle will look much longer and thinner. Do the same with the right corner (it will overlap) and then exactly the same thing with the top corners.

5. Take the top and bottom corners and fold them in to the middle.

6. Here is the tricky part - you'll need to open your boat up. Grab all the folds together from one side and pull up and the same with the other. Once you have done this, carefully turn your boat inside out. This may take a little practice but you'll get it in the end.

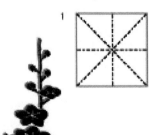   

Summer Spiral

These look beautiful hanging from trees or in the garden. Cut along the spiral line then hang from a piece of thread from the middle.

Why not turn the spiral over and create your own words and design?

CHINESE DRAGON

Dragons have been in Chinese mythology and folklore for thousands and thousands of years. They appear in art, stories, jewelry, decorations, clothing, there are dragon boat races and dragon dancing (life sized dragon puppets at key events such as New Year). The dragon symbolises strength, power and good luck. Dragons are strong, confident, self-assured, brave, passionate and creative.

You can be powerful like a Dragon. What type of dragon would you like to be.

How to make your Chinese Dragon: Carefully cut out the dragon body parts on the page and colour them in. On coloured paper, draw around your hands about 10 or 15 times and carefully cut them out. Write a positive quality on each hand. Overlap the hands (facing the same direction) to build the dragon's body, you could make the hands go up and down slightly to give the body a more snake like shape. Glue the hands together how you have positioned them. Stick into place the dragon head, tail and legs.

relax Kids

www.relaxkids.com

Animal Track Memory Game

Cut out all the sqaures. Turn them all over, upside down so that you can't see them. Mix the cards up so you can't remember what the cards are. Now you are ready to play. Turn over any 2 cards - if they match, set them aside and try match another pair. If they don't match, turn them back over and try again. Keep going until you've matched all the animal tracks.

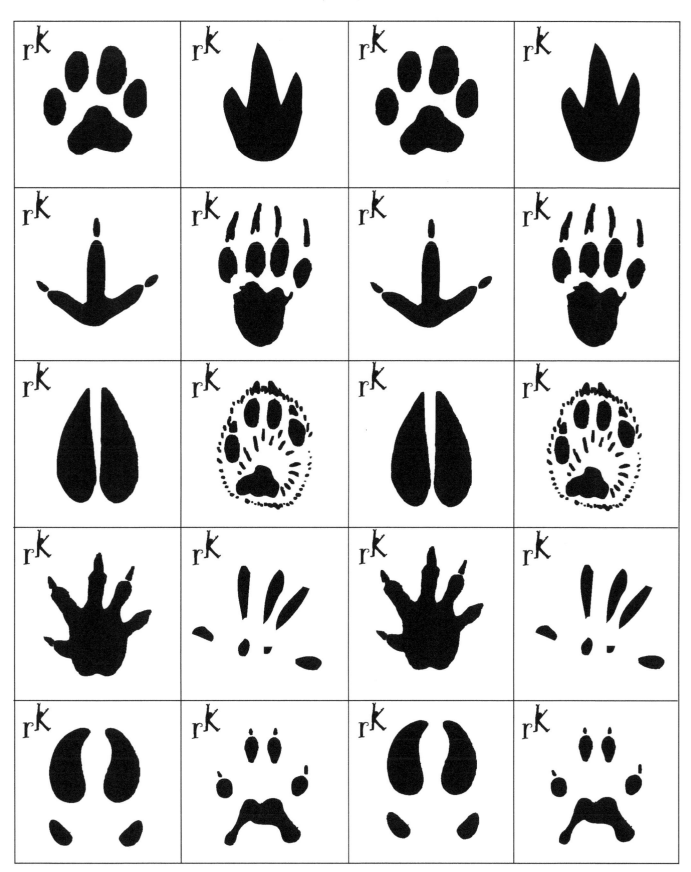

WORRY MONSTERS

WHAT TO DO:

Cut out your little
monsters and write down
your worries. Place them
in a box and let your
monsters nibble away at
your worries.

relax Kids
www.relaxkids.com

www.relaxkids.com

www.relaxkids.com

www.relaxkids.com

www.relaxkids.com

www.relaxkids.com

relax Kids

Wheel of life

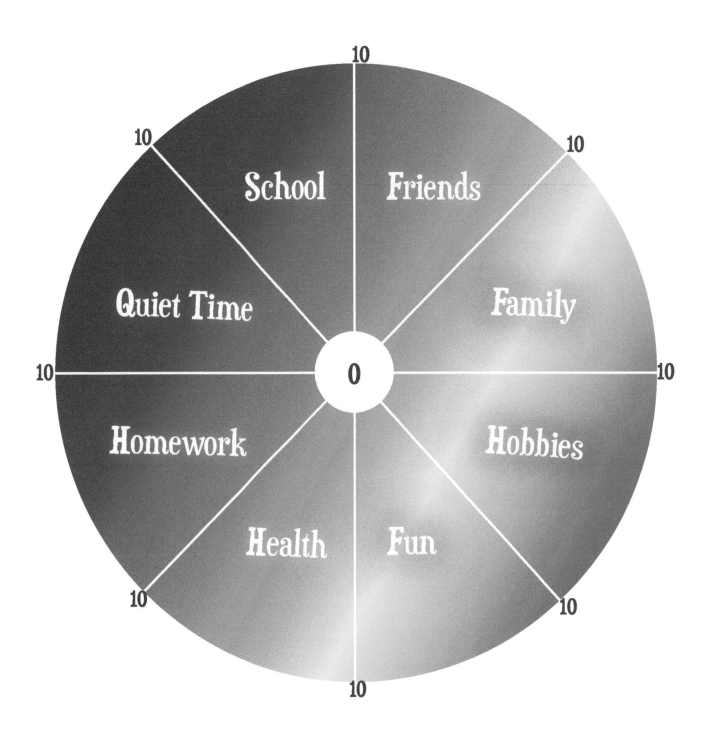

It is important to have a balanced life.
Check each section and make a mark to show how happy you feel about that part of your life (on a scale of 0-10)
Once you have filled in each section, look at how you can improve some parts of your life.

FREE

positive thoughts

from **relax Kids**

www.relaxkids.com

please take one

today i will be step into
my own power

today i will remain
calm no matter what

today i will look after
myself with care

today i will be positive
and bright

today i will believe
in myself

today i will cherish my
body and soul

today i will conserve
my energy

today i will be step into
my own power

today i will remain
calm no matter what

today i will look after
myself with care

today i will be positive
and bright

fantastic calm

COOL BRAVE

unique Magical

STRONG

thoughtful caring

AMAZING Lovely

Chill Super

tranquil special

peaceful

Colour these in and use them to decorate folders, boxes, pencil cases or whatever you like!

relax Kids

www.relaxkids.com

I wish you... **Joy**
relax kids
www.relaxkids.com

I wish you... **Love**
relax kids

I wish you... **Strength**
relax kids
www.relaxkids.com

I wish you... **Confidence**
relax kids
www.relaxkids.com

I wish you... **Power**
relax kids

I wish you... **Health**
relax kids
www.relaxkids.com

I wish you... **Abundance**
relax kids

I wish you... **Contentment**
relax kids
www.relaxkids.com

I wish you... **Cheer**
relax kids
www.relaxkids.com

I wish you... **Happiness**
relax kids

I wish you... **Energy**
relax kids

I wish you... **Peace**
relax kids

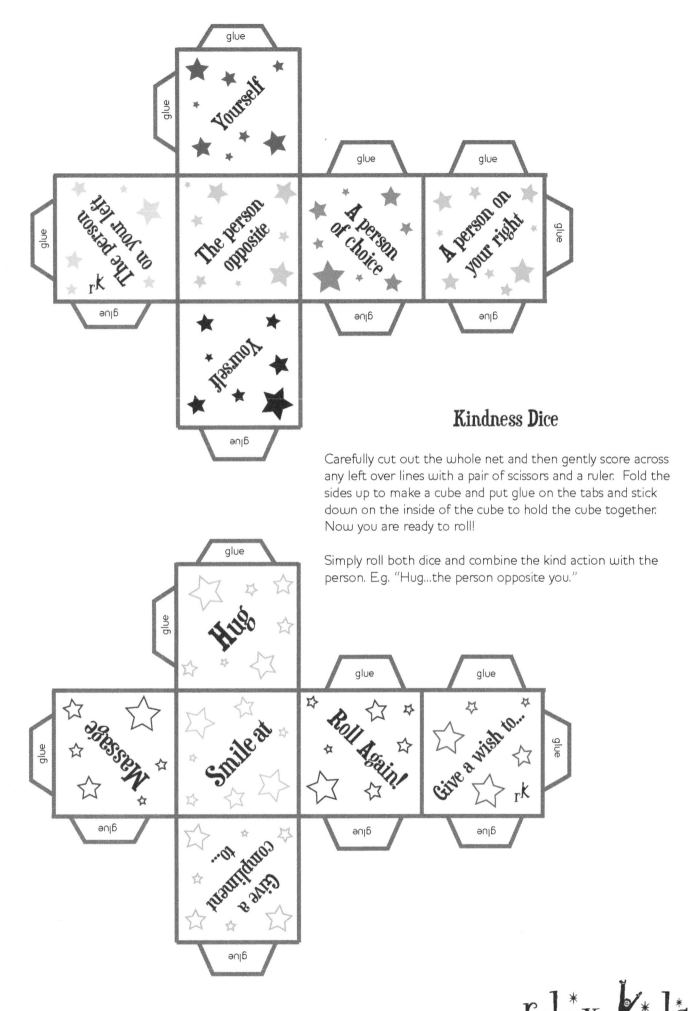

Kindness Dice

Carefully cut out the whole net and then gently score across any left over lines with a pair of scissors and a ruler. Fold the sides up to make a cube and put glue on the tabs and stick down on the inside of the cube to hold the cube together. Now you are ready to roll!

Simply roll both dice and combine the kind action with the person. E.g. "Hug...the person opposite you."

relax Kids

www.relaxkids.com

How to make relaxing dough

You will need:
- half a cup of flour
- half a cup of salt
- 2tbsp cream of tartar
- a cup of water
- food coloring

Play dough is so good for de-stressing. You get to make it into nice shapes and pictures or just give it a good squeeze to make yourself feel calmer. It's nice when you make it with your mum or dad or someone older, because they can do all the tricky bits that kids can't and you get to chat with them while you do it.

1. Mix the flour, salt and cream of tartar with a cup of water until you get a paste.

2. Get an adult to heat the mixture over a warm hob until it sticks together like dough.

3. Then, split the dough into a few pieces and add a few drops of the food coloring to make bright colors. We usually make yellow, red and blue, because then you can mix those colors up to make new ones.

4. To make the dough extra good for de-stressing, add a couple of drops of essential oil to make it smell nice. Lavender oil is good to help you sleep. Eucalyptus oil is good if you have a cold. Mandarin oil is good if you feel stressed.

5. You can do what you want with the dough. I like getting the different colors and winding bits together to make snail shells and things like that!

6. It sounds silly but whenever we have done something like this, I feel really confident because I have made something from nothing and I have done it from scratch. I love my lavender dough the best!

I am relaxed. I am relaxed.

I am

www.relaxkids.com

Fill in each petal with a positive word to describe yourself.
See if you can fill the whole flower.

CAT & MOUSE

One player is Cats and one player is Mouse. Players need to take turns to place a Cat or Mouse on the grid. However, they can only be in squares that are joined by a corner. The last player who places a card card on the board is the winner.

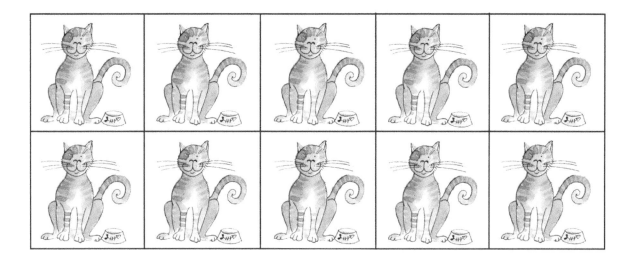

Carefully cut out the Cat and Mouse tokens.

www.relaxkids.com

Wishing Star

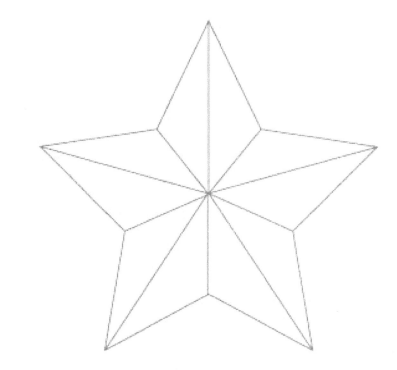

1.

Fold your square piece of paper in half from the bottom, up.

2.

Fold the bottom right corner to the top edge and unfold again

3.

Fold the top right down to the bottom edge and unfold.

4.

Fold the bottom left corner to the middle point of the folded cross on the right

5.

Using the piece you have just folded, take the right corner and fold over to the left to line up with the left edge

6.

Take the bottom right corner and fold so that the bottom edge meets and lines up with the centre fold

7.

Fold in half backwards from the centre fold

Why not make your wishes hang from the ceiling or turn them into hanging Christmas Tree decorations by tying a loop of string or pretty ribbon through one point of the star

8.

Carefully cut from the right corner down to make a triangle (see pic)

Unfold the triangle to reveal your star.

Snowflake Game

This is a game for 2 or more players - you will need a snowflake each and one die.

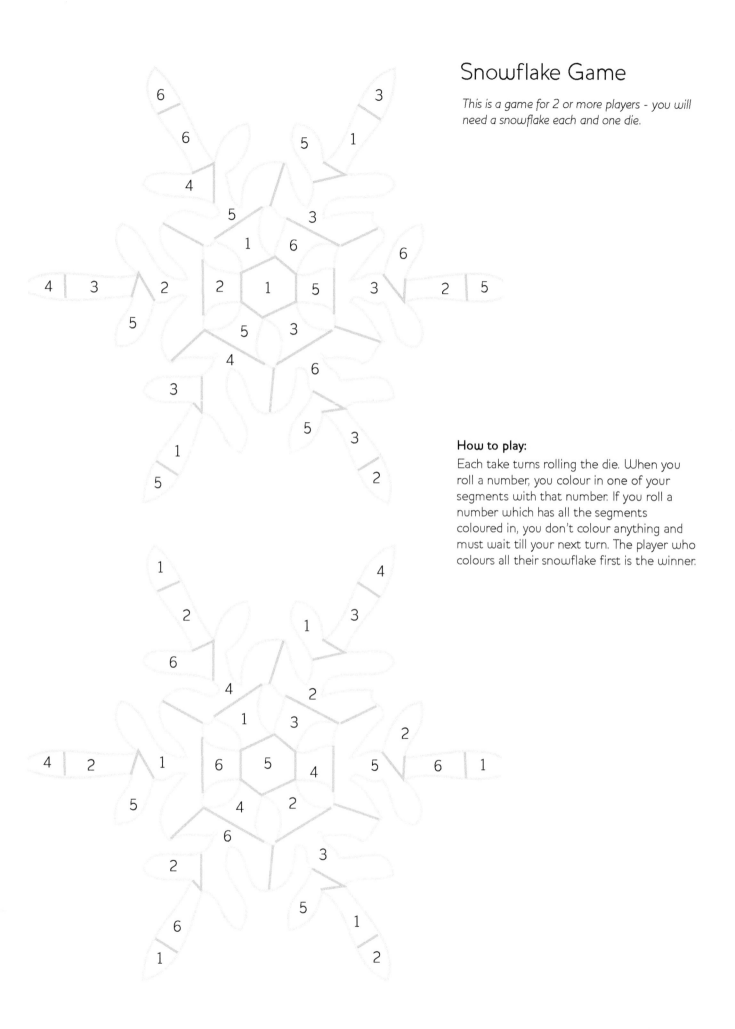

How to play:

Each take turns rolling the die. When you roll a number, you colour in one of your segments with that number. If you roll a number which has all the segments coloured in, you don't colour anything and must wait till your next turn. The player who colours all their snowflake first is the winner.

relax Kids

www.relaxkids.com

101 things to do when you're bored

Cut these out, fold them up and place them all in an empty jar or something similar. Whenever your feeling bored, simply pull one out of the jar for a solution to your boredem.

Lie down and look up at the clouds	Make someone smile
Gaze up at the stars at night	Start a fun craft project
Dance to music	Explore the garden or park.
Go for a bike ride	Sculpt something out of tin foil
Doodle	Copy a famous painting
Arm wrestle with your dad	Run up and down the stairs as many times as you can
Play 'Rock, Paper, Scissors'	Plant seeds and watching them grow
Say a word and find all the words that rhyme with it	Camp in the garden
Play 'I Spy'	Breathe in and out deeply and slowly
Walk around the block and pick up as much litter as you can find	Blow bubbles
Make macaroni necklaces	Watch TV without the sound and make up the soundtrack
Make popcorn	Create your own magazine
Make a family tree	Record your own Radio
Make mud pies	Make dolls clothes
Make up a scavenger hunt	Play outside in the rain
Tidy your room	Write a Haiku poem
Make handmade cards for special people	Wear your clothes backwards
Play hopscotch	Make a time capsule and bury it in the garden
Teach your dog a new trick	Do a huge jigsaw puzzle
Thumb wrestle	Blink really fast and enjoy the light show
Play with someone's hair	Make a list 20 things you like yourself
Write silly songs	Make a list 20 things you like about your friends and family
Write in a notebook	Play music on pots and pans
Learn and practice Morse Code	Paint a picture of your house
Make a den	Write a letter to yourself to keep it for your 21st birthday
Laugh at least 40 times a day	Try not to speak for the whole day or an hour!

101 things to do when you're bored

Cut these out, fold them up and place them all in an empty jar or something similar. Whenever your feeling bored, simply pull one out of the jar for a solution to your boredem.

Write a story that is less than 100 words	Make someone laugh
Have a proper tea party with cups and tea cakes and little sandwiches	Put one hand behind your back and manage with just one arm
Follow an ant around the garden	Get a back rub
Draw a life-sized picture of yourself	Have a water fight
Write a letter for people in the future and let them know what it is like to be you	Play charades
Build a fairy house in the garden	Write 'I am wonderful' 20 times
Make a scrap book	Pretend you are on a beach in the living room
Draw a map of the house and garden	Make up stories
Put on a play	Climb trees
Invent a secret code	Film your own TV show
Give and get a hand massage	Make things out of scrap and rubbish
Write a poem	Dress up and pretend you someone else
Learn a card trick	Go on a wildlife safari and finding all the wildlife near you
Have a bubble bath	Hug trees
Interview a grown up	Design a poster
Practice Origami	Put on a singing show
Read your favourite book	Collect something
Watch people and see if you can make up stories about them	Feed and watch the birds
Talk to your parents and grandparents about your ancestors	Set up a stall and sell things you have made
Try a tongue twister	Make a collage out of photos
Speak in gibberish and make up a language	Stretch - see how many different shapes you can make
Make a list of your favourite things in the world	Make a list 20 things you like about your friends and family
Close your eyes and count 60 seconds.	
Draw a letter on your friend's back and see if they can guess what it is	
Have a staring contest with a friend	
Pick a letter and say all the things that begin with that letter	

Be a Star Today!
How many can you tick off

☐ Beautiful Star – For helping someone else feel good about themselves

☐ Bright Star – For working hard

☐ Brilliant Star – For doing something amazing

☐ Calm Star – For staying cool under pressure

☐ Carefree Star – For not letting your worries bother you

☐ Co-Operative Star – For a team player

☐ Confident Star – For an act of leadership

☐ Creative Star – For doing something artistic

☐ Dancing Star – For moving with style

☐ Courageous Star – For bravery

☐ Determined Star – For being dedicated to something

☐ Enthusiastic Star – For putting your whole heart into what you do

☐ Forgiving Star – For accepting someone else's mistake

☐ Friendly Star – For making a new friend

☐ Generous Star – For an act of giving

☐ Happy Star – For being positive

☐ Healthy Star – For being active

☐ Helpful Star – For lending a hand

☐ Honest Star – For telling the truth

☐ Joyful Star – For being cheerful

☐ Kind Star – For doing something nice for someone else

☐ Lovely Star – For being sweet

☐ Loving Star – For being caring

☐ Magic Star – For surprising someone with a thoughtful moment

☐ Peaceful Star – For a relaxed person

☐ Responsible Star – For being sensible

☐ Sharing Star – For offering something to someone else

☐ Smiling Star – For sharing their happiness

☐ Still Star – For being content

☐ Super Star – For being a hero/ heroine

☐ Talented Star – For learning a new skill

☐ Truthful Star – For being sincere

☐ Wise Star – For being mature

☐ Wonderful Star – For doing something super

☐ Respectful Star – For being well mannered and gracious

relax Kids

Treasure Chest Maze

Can you help the merman find the treasure chest before the fish get to it..?

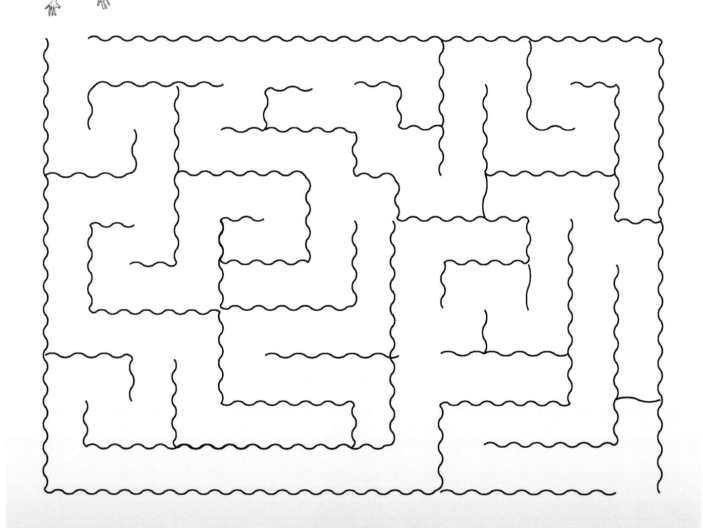

www.relaxkids.com

Key:
Happy and positive - yellow
Sad/upset - brown
Calm and peaceful - green
Energetic - orange
Angry - red

Mood Tree

relax Kids

www.relaxkids.com

This is your mood tree. It has 365 leaves - one for each day of the year. Colour in each leaf depending on how you feel that day when you wake up or before you go to bed. The mood tree is a great way of recording how your moods change each day. In a years time, you will be able to track and see how you felt each day.

We hope you enjoy your mood tree.

OUR STREET
BOOKS

Our Street Books for children of all ages, deliver a potent mix of
fantastic, rip-roaring adventure and fantasy stories to excite the
imagination; spiritual fiction to help the mind and the heart
grow; humorous stories to make the funny bone grow; historical
tales to evolve interest; and all manner of subjects that stretch
imagination, grab attention, inform, inspire and keep the pages
turning. Our subjects include Non-fiction and Fiction, Fantasy
and Science Fiction, Religious, Spiritual, Historical, Adventure,
Social Issues, Humour, Folk Tales and more.